LOOKING BACK AT CLASS 24 & 25 LOCOMOTIVES

LOOKING BACK AT CLASS 24 & 25 LOCOMOTIVES

Full house at Barmouth, with Nos 24082, 24133, 25101 and 25253 all rattling away as they await passengers for their return excursions on 5 June 1977 for Her Majesty's Silver Jubilee. (Steve Burdett)

Kevin Derrick

AMBERLEY

This edition first published 2016

Amberley Publishing
The Hill, Stroud
Gloucestershire, GL5 4EP

www.amberley-books.com

Copyright © Kevin Derrick, 2016

The right of Kevin Derrick to be identified as
the Author of this work has been asserted in
accordance with the Copyrights, Designs and
Patents Act 1988.

ISBN 978 1 4456 6043 1 (print)
ISBN 978 1 4456 6044 8 (ebook)

British Library Cataloguing in Publication Data.
A catalogue record for this book is available from
the British Library.

Typesetting by Amberley Publishing.
Printed in the UK.

Contents

Introduction

We take another look within the *Looking Back At* series at the British Railways-designed Type 2 designs, which would emerge over an eight-year period from the works of Derby, Crewe and Darlington and from outside contractors Beyer Peacock at Gorton. The first deliveries began from Derby Works in the summer of 1958 with a pilot batch of twenty locomotives in theory for the London Midland Region as part of the Modernisation Plan.

However, the Southern Region started to borrow a number of these new arrivals pending the delivery of the BRCW Type 3s and the delayed start-up of parts of the Kent electrification scheme in their rush to eliminate steam.

Above: One of the tablet catcher recess fitted Class 25s, D7619 runs through West Hampstead on the former Midland Railway's mainline in April 1969. (Grahame Wareham)

This page: Lingering around Leicester depot and station area on 22 February 1969 was D5183. (George Woods)

Their use on the Southern Region was not without problems; as with a number of the early classes the Derby-built Type 2s were found to be overweight, in this case almost five tons! This heavier than expected axle loading was a major concern for the Southern Region's Civil Engineer, leading to D5004 and D5005 visiting Eastleigh Works in February 1959 to see what could be done to reduce their axle loadings. The easiest solution was to remove the train-heating boiler and boiler water tanks, this being done on locomotives D5002–D5006, which made them a little more versatile in regard to their route availability, though the boilers must have been missed during the winter months.

The Civil Engineers eased their restrictions affecting the overweight Type 2s, most returned to the LMR to have the boilers and water tanks refitted during 1960, whilst deliveries continued from Derby, Crewe and Darlington of production locomotives for the London Midland and Eastern Regions. The design was being upgraded through this time, whilst outside contractors' locomotives were proving even less desirable to British Railways.

In 1962 the Southern's promised BRCW Type 3s began arriving, coupled with the successful start up of the Kent electrification plan the borrowed Type 2s were slowly returned to the London Midland Region. By now British Railways were firmly committed to their own design of Type 2s resulting in further orders and improvements, culminating with the delivery of the last one D7677 from Derby Works on 29 April 1967.

After twenty-nine years their service careers were to come to a close although several lingered on as Ethels. Leaving behind a legacy of a mix of twenty-four locomotives from Classes 24 and 25 for preservationists to keep from the clutches of ever hungry scrap dealers in the future. As with the remaining books in this series we deal with each classes active working life and disposal, leaving the preservation stories to the popular railway magazines to document.

Kevin Derrick

Class 24 Variants

At least four of the Sulzer-engined 1,160-hp locomotives are on shed in north London Hornsey on 11 February 1962, with D5067 and D5068 identifiable. Ironically both would fail to make it to be renumbered into TOPS due to accident damage, leaving them both to be cut up during 1973. (Rail Online)

Whilst the first of these Type 2s went into service in the summer of 1958, many would sadly only enjoy short service careers. This example D5029 finds employment still at Crewe during August 1971 which had now become a stronghold for many of its classmates. However, it already exhibits signs of a reduced desire to maintain the class with the absence of some of the lower side panels. (Grahame Wareham)

Having survived periods in store already, No. 24073 was enjoying a final spree of workings at Croes Newydd on 3 March 1977, however it was cut up the following year. (Strathwood Library Collection)

Helping out a failed DMU passenger service along the Cambrian Coast at Tywyn on 22 July 1967 was D5006 from the initial pilot batch of locomotives with the divided radiator side grills. (Bill Wright)

In April 1973, No. 5080 heads a ballast working past Llynlys near Oswestry as the first signs of spring are in the trees. (Rail Photoprints)

Deliveries of the more powerful 1,250-hp Sulzer-engined versions began in April 1960 with D5114, these were easily identifiable by the fitting of roof-mounted four-character headcode boxes as here on D5134, stabled at Crewe on 21 September 1969. The split pattern radiator grill must have been swapped from one of the twenty pilot 1,160-hp locomotives during a works visit. (Rail Online)

Visits to Derby Works for overhauls often meant adaptions, such as here with No. 24055, one of the lower-powered production Class 24s at Walsall in September 1976 with one cab from one of the later builds as above, and now having been stripped of all of the lower bodyside panels to ease maintenance. Also compare the water tank with the locomotive above. (Rail Online)

Above and below: Back to the second-built of the pilot locomotives, which was stored out of use and posted as withdrawn when this view was taken at Crewe South in August 1969. It would be reinstated that October for another six years' use before laying out idle again to be scrapped at Doncaster Works in late 1977. From the production batch D5111 passes Shap Summit at the head of a Blackpool–Newcastle service on 15 July 1967. (Photos: Grahame Wareham & Chris Davies/Rail Photoprints)

The last active Class 24 became a favourite for cameramen and British Rail alike in its latter days appearing at a number of open days. The final date for No. 24081 in service was 5 October 1980, however it had already been acquired for preservation, initially at Steamport in Southport. As part of its charmed existence, it displays a few extra painted details as it approaches the level crossing at Brymbo Middle Signal Box. This steeply graded branch supplied the former large steelworks in the village of Brymbo near Wrexham, on 14 September 1979. The blast furnaces here were in operation between 1796 and closure which took place in 1990. (John Arthur Bennett/Strathwood Library Collection)

Both this example, No. 24065 at Millerhill in July 1976, and No. 24081, seen opposite, have had their draughty front connecting doors plated over during works visits. However, the headcode discs and lamps have been centred up now on this Haymarket-allocated machine. Spells in storage at Cadder Yard, Carstairs, Haymarket and here at Millerhill were inflicted upon No. 24065 during 1975 and 1976. Eventually it went south to Swindon Works and perished with a number of its classmates at the hands of the scrappers who it seemed to prefer cutting these Type 2s rather than their beloved Westerns. (Alan Rintoul)

This is how the gangway connecting doors looked on the later 1,250-hp locomotives such as D5116 in just its second week of service based out of 60A Inverness whilst on a goods train at Aviemore on 15 June 1960. This was one of the first batch from D5114 to D5132 built at Derby Works which were ordered for use in the Highlands; these were all specified with a tablet-catcher recess, although the catchers themselves only started to be fitted after October 1960 on visits to St Rollox. Note the extra footplate staff in the cab, no doubt learning the new Type 2s. (Frank Hornby)

Whilst staff as Inverness and St Rollox sought to seal off those draughty front doors during the latter part of the sixties, examples such as No. 24137, which went to the London Midland Region at Longsight when new, would end their days with them still possibly operable if staff fought their way through the layers of paint to open them. Withdrawn from active service out of Crewe in the summer of 1976, No. 24137 was stored at Bescot from May 1976 until January 1978, when it was towed here to Toton for use in re-railing exercises as an organised party of spotters make a visit on misty 14 Janaury 1978. It was towed, somewhat battered, to Swindon Works on 25 July that year for cutting up during October 1978. (Steve Burdett)

Perhaps it was ironic that Inverness and many other Scottish depots switched to the use of one number and dots in the headcode boxes during the 1960s to identify trains, as here with D5139 at Laurencekirk with an Aberdeen–Perth on 27 May 1966. (Strathwood Library Collection)

Use on the remote and lengthy single-track sections on the Far North Lines-led Inverness depot to fit both its Class 24s and Class 26s with twin headlights, both to see the many unprotected crossings and any animals on the line would be startled along with the drivers as they hove into view at night and in bad weather. This is tablet-catcher-fitted No. 5126 at Georgemas Junction station on 15 October 1971. (George Woods)

All of these Inverness-allocated locomotives on this page and opposite carry three-piece snowploughs and the ventilated style of side-grill covers as here with No. 5130 in August 1971 on its home shed, the headcode glasses were also beefed up to protect them from the weather. (Grahame Wareham)

The Highlands' preferred attempts at sealing off the connecting doors was to use strips of steel beading, whilst D5115 stands in Inverness yard to the south of the station with an engineers train on 28 April 1973 (Paul Townsend)

Class 25 Improvements

The first-built of what became Class 25, D5151, which entered service from Darlington Works on 15 April 1961, is seen attached to a brake tender at the head of coal train at Newburn Junction in March 1967. (Colour Rail)

Ready for service in the sunshine at Darlington Works on 1 April 1962 was D5184. The first twenty-five of this improved design were intended for freight use, as such they did not carry train-heat boilers or water tanks, whilst D5176 onwards recieved the final variation of fuel and water tanks where boilers were to be fitted. They also were now fitted with a single style of battery tray per side as opposed to the previous two-tray arrangement. (Strathwood Libray Collection)

Top speed for the Class 24 designs was limited to 75 mph, while these improved Type 2s, later classified as Class 25s, would reach 90 mph. Thornaby-allocated D5163 has returned to its birthplace Darlington Works for attention on 23 March 1963. (Colour Rail)

A move away from its first depot at Thornaby to Holbeck had been made for Darlington-built D5172 by the time it was recorded at Bolton-le-Sands on 10 July 1968 lending a hand to Black Five No. 45134 in the last weeks of steam in the North West. (George Woods)

The next production batch D5186 to D5222 would emerge from Derby Works with D5187 seen here at Nottingham's steam shed on 31 March 1965. Having entered service on 23 March 1963, this was before Darlington had completed their order on 25 May 1963 with D5185 to 18A Toton. (Bill Wright)

Construction of a further batch D7578 to D7597 to this revised design was allocated to Darlington Works before it later closed for the London Midland Region. Visually these and the Derby-built locomotives had revised headcode boxes, external hinges and an overlap to connecting doors, whilst the cabside doors were recessed now, with changes to their handrails. Also the lower bodyside flaps and bufferbeam valances were cleaned up. Displaying these modifications at Polmadie in August 1971 for us was D7587. (Grahame Wareham)

Above and below: The former D7569 from this revised Darlington batch became No. 25219 under TOPS in May 1974. By the time of this view at Cardiff Canton on 30 June 1979, the connecting doors had been sealed up during a works visit; it was withdrawn from service officially on 6 April 1983, while sister No. 25218 is running without its headcode glass at the leading end near Bescot in June 1982. (Photos: Brian Daniels & David T. Williams)

Above and below: All four locomotives in this spread have differing arrangements for their lamp brackets and headboard clips after these door modifications with No. 25049 at Gleneagles on 28 May 1977 and No. 25080 on the Hayle branch on 13 September two years later. (Photos: George Woods & Bob Dibley)

Above and below: The uprated design was cleaned up again to remove the gangway doors and move the side intake grills to the roof cantrail. Locomotives using this modified shell would be produced from both Derby Works and Beyer Peacock, this is No. 25194 at New Street in June 1981 and No. 25269 at Lawrence Hill, Bristol on 20 May 1978. (Photos: David T. Williams & Rail Photoprints)

This new design enjoyed improved cab layouts for the engine crews, here being explored by visitors to the Reading Depot open day on 1 June 1985. Originally numbered as D7652, it became No. 25302 February 1974. (Bob Dibley)

As these later production orders were destined for freight duties, most were built without train-heating equipment, leaving a great void underneath the bodywork – as shown with these locomotives including No. 25115 awaiting banking duties at Manchester Victoria on 22 September 1982. (Peter Brackenbury)

Paired up for this working on 20 June 1967, along with at least three brake vans to perhaps aid with pulling them up on this steep route, are D7651 and D7540 as they near Rose Grove. (George Woods)

Listed as allocated to the LMML pool when seen at Cricklewood in August 1967 was D7519, it was new on 9 January 1965 and sent to 16A Toton. (Grahame Wareham)

The former D5286, now running as No. 25136, would need all of its haulage and braking ability too on this turn as it runs through Chinley with a Peak Forest–Northwich ICI limestone train on 5 September 1981. (Rail Photoprints)

London Division D01-based D7562 pauses at Nuneaton Trent Valley on 28 June 1967 with a parcels working, showing the original placing of the worksplates under the cab windows. (Strathwood Library Collection)

Whereas D7601, now running as No. 25251, shows the bolt holes for the original fixing but its worksplate is now curiously affixed to the cab door when seen at Willesden on 15 July 1977. (Colin Whitbread)

Another good load to contend with for Springs Branch–allocated No. 25172, as it approaches Guide Bridge with a Tunstead–Northwich limestone service on 27 September 1979. The locomotive was new into service on 9 January 1965 and was withdrawn on 1 February 1981 after what must be regarded as an all too brief working life. (Rail Photoprints)

Stabled Quietly

Much of the rubble has been swept into the inspection pits from the former roundhouse at Leeds Holbeck, as No. 5112 nestles among her sisters on what was her home shed at the time on 13 July 1969. (Rail Photoprints)

In its Tamworth Castle guise, No. 25322 keeps the baby Sulzer sound alive during the summer of 1985 at Cricklewood after all her classmates had been swept away from London. Eight other Class 25s gained white-painted unofficial Castle or Welsh spelling Castell names at Aberystwyth in late 1986 and early 1987, added to their flanks onto a mock black painted background, whilst retaining their often scruffy blue liveries. (Brian Daniels)

It was the influx of Class 25s in the early 1970s that swept away the Class 22s from Devon and Cornwall and their hold on china-clay traffic from here at St Blazey where we see No. 25052 on 24 July 1980. (Brian Daniels)

Whilst in Scotland, the Sulzer sounds were shared with a fleet of Class 26s & Class 27s, as by the time of this view on 17 April 1978 at Perth, all of the Class 24s had been purged from the Highlands. (Brian Daniels)

Just a couple of years beforehand we cound enjoy sights such as No. 24107 in the sun at Motherwell, the pipework for working the Consett iron-ore traffic still affixed to its bufferbeam in August 1976, two months later this locomotive went into store at Millerhill, never to work again. (Rail Photoprints)

Whereas the damage to the cab of No. 25051, stopped at Old Oak Common on its way to Works on 23 March 1979, would be repaired and returned to service out of Bescot. (Brian Daniels)

A fine portrait of the former D7608 after renumbering into TOPS as No. 25258 in April 1974. At this time we all had to keep referring back to our Ian Allan ABCs to work out whether we had seen the locomotive before or not! This view shows the locomotive in the depot yard at Willesden in September 1978, it was a bit of a stranger here really, being based out of Toton for most of the decade. It would go to Springs Branch in November 1980 before joining many of the last survivors based out of Crewe in October 1982. When withdrawal did come, it was stored at Carlisle to await the call of the breakers. (G. W. Sharpe Collection)

Associated for a number of years with the Cambrian lines, Class 24s such as No. 24087 would be forced to share what was left of the former steam shed at Machynlleth with area's DMU fleet as here on 7 July 1974. (Steve Burdett)

While it is in the shelter of 133 tons of Class 40 such as No. 40191 that the 75 tons of No. 24035 takes cover alongside in Shrewsbury's loco sidings on 29 August 1977. (Steve Burdett)

Shut outside in the cold at Tyseley on Valentine's Day in 1982 and looking unloved was the recently withdrawn No. 25156; the following month it was sent to Swindon Works, who scrapped it completely by the end of that May. (Brian Daniels)

Elsewhere in Birmingham we see No. 25040 at Saltley during the late 1970s. Withdrawn in November 1980 this locomotive would also head for Swindon Works and would be broken up less than a week before the shot above of No. 25156 was taken. (Nev Sloper)

Another Birmingham depot to see Class 25 action, and in earlier years Class 24 action too, was Bescot, where we find No. 25272 and No. 25203 taking in the sunshine alongside the former steam shed here in May 1980. (David T. Williams)

The summer sunshine also picks out the unkempt condition of D5059 at Crewe during August 1969, several of its classmates had already been in storage pending decisions about their futures at this time before they were reprieved. (Grahame Wareham)

In contrast, D5225, allocated at the time to the LMML pool, is recently ex-works from here at Derby in April 1967. It does highlight a common problem, however, to all of these baby Sulzers with the ultimate erosion of their paintwork due to a reaction between a coolant additive and the paint. This was caused by overfilling the coolant system as the vent was on the roof. Not at all due radiator failures, they would always seemed more prone to this than many other classes that had roof-mounted vents and relief valves. (Mike Jefferies/Rail Photoprints)

The first locomotive with the revised body shape to be delivered was D5234 on 14 December 1963, beating D5233 (seen here) into traffic by a week. Just these first five, D5233 to D5237, were fitted with steam-heat boilers. With big brother Sulzer power from 1786 and D1857 in this view at Wellingborough on 21 June 1970, we can see how the paintwork on D5233 has been touched up due to this overfilling of coolant problem. (Gordon Edgar)

The flowers of the rosebay willowherb have gone over as we find D5269 stabled among the Class 20s in the depot yard at Burton-on-Trent during August 1969. Renumbered as No. 25119, this locomotive was destined to be the last Class 25 allocated to Toton depot, after a working career of twenty-one years, in June 1985. After withdrawal, No. 25119 was stored at Basford Hall Yard in Crewe until it was moved to Doncaster Works on 16 April 1986 in the company of fellow condemned Class 25s No. 25044, Nos 25226 and 25245 as the 9Z34 Crewe–Warrington–Doncaster Works, with the former D5269 being scrapped within Doncaster Works by the middle of July 1986. (Grahame Wareham)

When D7532 was seen standing in the rows outside Toton during August 1971 she had just over thirteen more years' use ahead of her. Renumbered as No. 25182, she was withdrawn during January 1985. Over 25–27 March, in the company of No. 08095, she was moved from Toton to Swindon, picking up Nos 25076 and 25218 along the way at Bescot for scrapping. (Grahame Wareham)

The remains of the former steam shed at Haymarket are being pulled down around an ex-works D5159 in this view from 10 May 1966. The locomotive had been new from Darlington Works in July 1961, being sent to take up service first of all from 51L Thornaby. (Class Twenty Locomotive Society)

Above: Another chance to play spot the difference between these two body-styles of Class 25s from Darlington and Derby Works as D5214 sits on shed at Cricklewood during April 1969. (Grahame Wareham)

Opposite: Fellow London Division regular D5220 shares stabling facilities with Class 45 Peaks at Cambridge Street in between duties to and from St Pancras on 4 July 1969. (Rail Photoprints)

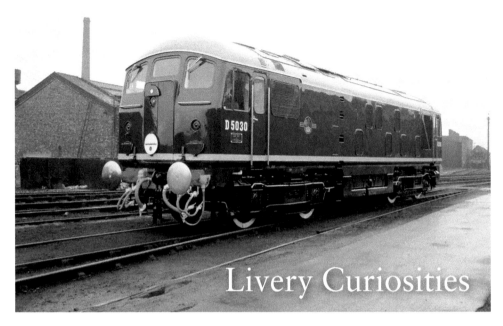

Livery Curiosities

Aside from D5000, which bore an off white side stripe when new, this is how all of the Class 24s went into traffic from Derby, Darlington and here at Crewe with their first-built posing for the cameras in May 1959. (Grahame Wareham Collection)

With trackside fatalies in mind, half-yellow warning panels were added from the early sixties to new build Class 25s and retro applied to Class 24s and the early build Class 25s. This shows how D5144 stands out against the background of Reddish Vale Viaduct on 30 April 1968. (George Woods)

Above and below: The unique stripey D5000 had gained its half-yellow panel by 3 September 1966 when seen on the last day of Great Central steam workings through Aylesbury. Note how some locomotives had rounded top corners to these yellow additions whilst others were squared off, as on D5037 in the washer at Ipswich in October 1966. This example, along with D5005, D5038, D5040 and D5053, also gained the later style of two-tone green livery during works visits to Derby during 1965. (Photos: George Woods & Rail Online)

Another Class 24 to have recieved a works visit during 1965 was D5025, which can be seen that August, climbing past Camden with a Down outer suburban service still showing a cleanish, light-grey roof and the standard as-built green livery with rounded yellow warning panels. Also of note is the white cantrail stripe dividing the roof and the green bodywork. (Dave Cobbe Collection/Rail Photoprints)

Above and below: The lower bodyside stripe has been painted over in green as has the British Railways emblem on pilot batch locomotive D5006, photographed at Crewe in August 1969. The roof may just be very dirty or could have been painted a darker grey or even dark green or black under all that grime. Likewise the lower body stripe has been painted out on D5113 seen at Grassington with a special on 16 June 1968, however the old style emblem has been replaced with Inter-City arrows. The upper white cantrail stripe is retained along with a grey roof scheme. This example was to wear unique half-yellow front panels along with arrows. (Photos: Grahame Wareham & Rail Photoprints)

Above and below: The painting of half-yellow warning panels shows further variation as it seems that when D5162 ran through Stockton on 13 November 1966 it had squared-off panels, whilst another view taken here on 18 May 1968 shows it with rounded top corners. (Both: Chris Davies/Rail Photoprints)

More wonders from Thornaby-based Class 25s as we see D5159 experimentally painted with an almost fluorescent orange warning panel departing from Tees Yard with a mixed freight on 17 April 1967. (Bill Wright)

Also seen the same day leaving Tees Yard was D5153, this time with a reflective light-yellow warning panel applied over the existing yellow, which now appears almost orange in comparison. Neither experiment was conclusive, the pair were first noted in these schemes in September 1966. (Bill Wright)

Opposite and above: Full-yellow ends were applied to the fleet from 1966/7, with D5231 found at Wellingborough on 21 June 1970. Comparison with D7587 at Burton the previous summer shows touch-ups of paint to the buffer beams, cab roofs and the cantrails appear or to be now either green or very dirty. Note how the yellow is stopped around the cab windows also. (Photos: Gordon Edgar & Grahame Wareham)

The depot painters have attacked No. 5071 in similar fashion, painting out the D-prefix and the old style emblem with green paint, most likely when they attended to the yellow front ends, again taken across the cantrail in this scene taken during September 1972 at Aberdeen Ferryhill. In addition, the central gangway has already been plated over and the discs centralised, although there is an issue with the yellow paint adhering to the new metalwork. (Grahame Wareham)

Another one for the notebooks, as by August 1969 D5092 was running light around the station limits at Crewe with a light-green bottom stripe and part of the upper cantrail stripe painted out in darker green whilst retaining the D-prefix, half-yellows and the old style emblem. For fans of livery variations this was a golden period right across the network for all manner of classes as there seemed to be no guidance to both works and depots on the desired new corporate livery. (Grahame Wareham)

Back at Crewe once again in July 1970 we find D5038, another of the two-tone green-liveried Class 24s, now, adorned with full-yellow ends and the painters have picked out the buffer beams with red paint in their enthusiasm. The locomotive is still in pretty much as-delivered condition: the frame-level skirts are still intact, the cab front gangway doors have not yet been sheeted over and the footsteps to the roof-mounted boiler water filler are still intact and not plated over, and here it is working under the overhead wires to boot. However, the old style British Railways emblems have been over-painted. (Grahame Wareham)

Further work with a green-filled paintbrush has improved the appearance of D5061 in this view taken at Crewe South on 20 March 1969, at a time when future work for them was in doubt. This time even the front valances and the cantrails are picked out in dark green, although in this sprucing-up attempt the painters have neglected to tidy up the headcode discs, must try harder! (Frank Hornby)

Another great comparison with attempts to revitalise the appearance of green-liveried Class 24s. Both Nos 5081 and 5031 have had their D-prefixes overpainted, whilst 5081 has gained a fresh coat of green, full yellow ends, grey roof, white cantrails all complete with a larger set of arrows, while No. 5031 has to make do with half-yellow fronts and the relief stripes painted out. The pair is seen rounding the curve from the North Wales line onto the Hooton line at Chester on 11 July 1971. (Strathwood Library Collection)

One further example of a Class 24 going into all-green for No. 5004 stopped at Eastfield in August 1971, the emblems etc. have all been over-painted. Also note that only the top two steps have been plated over to help prevent engine crews coming into accidental contact with overhead power lines while filling the boilers. (Grahame Wareham)

This time we can examine a Class 25 that has had the old-style emblem painted over but still retains the D-prefix when recorded at Toton in August 1971. It is also easy to see how far over the roof the brushes of the cleaning plant reach, whilst they seem to have little range around the front of the locomotive. (Grahame Wareham)

No. 5147 retains its emblem but has the D-prefix painted over in this view as the crew await to depart towards Glasgow once more from the old, now built-over, Fort William station on 3 August 1973. This Class 24/1 was also of her type fitted with the later style of winged headcode boxes, although they lacked the air horns fitted within, these remained fitted under the bufferbeams. (Strathwood Library Collection)

Seen back alongside the works at Derby after going out on test in May 1965, the brand-new D7549 displays the then standard livery for new-build Class 25s as part of a large batch of sixty-eight locomotives destined for the London Midland Region out of Toton. (Strathwood Library Collection)

Another batch built at Derby Works was for the Eastern Region and the Scottish Region. The latter's locomotives, D7611 to D7623, were built with tablet-catcher recesses, even though they do not seem to have been fitted at all. This is D7623, now in the D16 allocation based at Toton, having worked from here to Saltley in November 1969. (Grahame Wareham)

Another batch of fifty-four locomotives were awarded to Beyer Peacock, including D7625 here at Carnforth in April 1967, these subcontractors appear to have been placing the numbers slightly higher on the cabsides. Yes, this is another patch repaint due to overfilling the coolants. (Strathwood Library Collection)

This time another Class 25 ordered from the Beyer Peacock batch has had to be patch painted again with hardly a good match-up, while the British Railways emblem has been lost as well when seen outside the shed at Cricklewood on 20 April 1969. Whilst this locomotive was to have been built at Gorton, Beyer Peacock were in serious financial trouble. As a result of these problems, this once-much-respected company failed and went into bankruptcy. This forced the final eighteen locomotives from their original order of D7624–D7659 to be built at Derby Works by British Rail instead, as part of an order for the Eastern and London Midland Regions. (Dave Cobbe Collection/Rail Photoprints)

Some further patchwork painting on No. 7564, leading No. 7563 through Needham on 28 July 1973, has led to No. 7564 being recently transferred to Willesden to be sent out like this, complete with Inter-City arrows and a blue-painted frost-shield cover. (John Dawson)

One of the last green Class 25s to run with half-yellow front panels was No. 7647 seen here at Edge Hill. She was another patched locomotive and was to be only one of seventeen Class 25s to gain their TOPS number during 1973, the remainder being dealt with in 1974. Of note also is the dimple above the coupling hook to help ease use in service, a depot modification also applied to Class 33s too. (Steve Ireland)

At least twenty-one Class 25s made it through the TOPS renumbering process of 1973/4 still in their green liveries; among these was No. 25260, seen on its home shed of Bescot. By now the original two-tone green paintwork was almost ten years old. (Sylvester Booth/Strathwood Library Collection)

Above: Signs of touch-ups adorn two more of Bescot's allocation of Class 25s to retain their green liveries when recorded in August 1974, with Nos 25252 and 25261 taking a rest at Wolverhampton High Level. Interestingly both locomotives show signs of having recent work to their cabside window frames with the paint being removed. The far locomotive, No. 25261, was one of those originally destined for Scotland and retains tablet-catcher recesses. (Strathwood Library Collection)

Opposite: Lurking around the back of Newton Heath depot on 6 March 1976 was No. 25102, coupled to the area's breakdown train having just been transferred to Longsight out of the large Toton pool that January. (Phil Bidwell)

Above, below and opposite: Some more variations upon green renumbered locomotives include No. 25043, with some odd size numbers also in March 1976, twenty-three months after being so treated when seen under the overall roof of Carlisle Citadel, while No. 24136 was recorded at Llandudno Junction in September 1975, also with a blue-painted boiler-room vent cover. However, No. 24092, seen at Warrington in June 1974, appears to have a full repaint including a set of large Inter-City arrows.
(Photos: George Woods, David Hayes & Rail Photoprints)

Two locomotives appear to have been sent to Brush at Loughborough for repairs in the mid sixties, D5021 and D5218, seen here at Cricklewood in April 1969, it was returned to traffic in blue with old-style emblems and rounded half-yellow fronts. (Grahame Wareham)

D5218 later went into conventional blue livery, No. 5021 gained full-yellow ends and its D-prefixes were painted over while retaining those earlier emblems right to the end, later recieving its TOPS numbers. We see the engine at Derby Works, Reddish and Manchester Victoria. (Photos: Paul Dalton, Nev Sloper & Strathwood Library Collection)

Above and below: Sent new from Derby Works into traffic in blue with half yellow fronts were D7660 and D7661 in late 1966, looking a bit tatty now was D7661 at Willesden in August 1969, showing the use of two arrows each side with two sets of later style numbers inboard of the cab doors. In contrast Inverness sees D5125 in July 1970, with smaller arrows on the doors, full yellow ends and old style numbers with D-prefix. Note the tablet catchers fitted for use on the Highland lines. (Both: Grahame Wareham)

A similar style is worn by D5068, which was the first Class 24 into the new blue livery in December 1966, although one set of arrows is affixed back to front. It is led by D5132, also in blue but with a centrally affixed larger arrow, as they head some North Sea pipeline traffic at Huntley on 23 May 1967. (Late Dougie Grey/Strathwood Library Collection)

Two further Scottish Region variations at Inverness in August 1971, with D5117 affixed with small arrows, stabled in the ranks along the side of the engine shed in the sunshine. (Grahame Wareham)

An almost carbon copy is provided by No. 5115 on the same day, except the D-prefix has been dropped. Both locomotives are dressed in full Highland dress, vented boiler room covers, snow ploughs, headlights, tablet catchers, headcode glass covers, plated-over boiler access steps etc. (Grahame Wareham)

Full-yellow ends down to the buffers, newer styles of numbers with D-prefixes, along with two sets of larger arrows per side are worn by D5099 hauling a scrap Black Five No. 45017 through Hest Bank on 27 July 1968. (Strathwood Library Collection)

Derby Works outshopped the last built Class 25s during late 1966 and early 1967 in this same style. This is D7668 at the fuelling point out the back of Willesden Depot in April 1970. (Grahame Wareham)

A change now as whilst 5105 has the later style of number the use of the D-prefix has been dropped. It has been finished from its last works visit with a more economic use of a single large arrow each side, and the numbers underneath the cabside windows in this August 1971 view at Glasgow Works. This is the only example we have found in this variation for a Class 24. (Grahame Wareham)

This was a much more commonplace livery variation for Class 25s as witnessed firstly by No. 7576 at Eastfield in September 1972. (Grahame Wareham)

The renumbering process into TOPS began in earnest for the Class 24 and Class 25 fleet during 1973. One of the last Class 25s to be released from Derby Works after overhaul in this same style was No. 7562 that August as part of the locally based Toton allocation. It would soon become No. 25212 in February 1974 and would return to Derby Works in 1978 to become one of the Class 25s to be fitted with dual-braking equipment to further their lifespans and usefulness. (Dave Cobbe Collection/Rail Photoprints)

Most examples simply had their old numbers painted over and new TOPS numbers overlaid in this style on No. 25225, halted at Par under a stormy sky on 17 October 1975. (George Woods)

Whereas Glasgow Works seems to have favoured renumbering locomotives such as No. 25235, now fitted with dual brakes with the number behind the No.1 end cab doors as here at Peak Forest on 7 September 1981. (Steve Burdett)

Glasgow Works' last repairs to one of the pilot batch of Class 24s was to No. 24009 during May and June 1975. Within a month, many Scottish Class 24s were placed into store, including this virtually ex-works locomotive. Fortunately No. 24009 was briefly returned to service although it looks out of use in this view in the snow at Carstairs. This locomotive would be the only Class 24 in this style of livery and be the last of this Pilot group to be retired, during July 1976. (Rail Online)

Having been tasked with bringing new stock for the Southern Region on 14 March 1985, long-term Scottish resident No. 25231 carries slightly larger numbers in this Glasgow Works style whilst stopped at Willesden South West Sidings. (Brian Daniels)

Two oddballs for the price of one here at Chester on 12 May 1979, as No. 25224 carries no arrows at all, and the next in line, No. 25273, is one of the tablet-catcher-recess batch, with the number placed further back. Also, No. 24112 ran briefly with cabside numbers like No. 25224 and arrows on the other end. (Brian Daniels)

Having been cleaned, the damaged paintwork has been filled and primed ready for the top coat here on the former No. 5183, ready for renumbering into No. 25033 at Derby Works in February 1974. The yellow paintwork has been applied and masked off for a clean edge against the blue. (Rail Online)

Variations exist on just how the full-yellow fronts are finished, compared with No. 25033 opposite 7579 has its yellow paint up onto the roof cantrail guttering after a recent works visit whilst photographed taking in the August sunshine outside Polmadie in 1971. (Grahame Wareham)

Not only with a large central arrow and new style numbers complete with D-prefix, but D5118 stabled at Inverness in July 1970 has its yellow front stopped short of the usual edges seen elsewhere. (Grahame Wareham)

Above: The far-end cab of No. 24081 has the yellow front carried around the front cabside window while the rearmost is fairly standard in this view from 13 May 1978 at Chester. (Brian Daniels)

Left and below: Both No. 25001, seen at Edinburgh Waverley, and No. 5084 at Birkenhead Mollington Street are still to be renumbered on 19 January 1974 show how the yellow paint was often carried down around the buffer valances. (Steve Burdett)

Several Class 24s and Class 25s were seen from time to time with numbers often crudely affixed to their fronts; one such example was No. 25181 seen on 12 March 1986 at Bangor. However, the former No. 24061 arose phoenix-like from the grave as RDB9680007, then metamorphosed into No. 97201, later named *Experiment* within the departmental stock as here at Cardiff Canton in 1985. It was enough to ensure its survival into preservation, thankfully. (Photos: Brian Daniels & Rail Photoprints)

Another interesting livery transition befell D7672 during its working career. Put into traffic as part of the D16 Nottingham Division based out of Toton on 25 February 1967, we catch up with it six weeks into its working life, already showing signs of wear and tear in the then-standard blue livery of the day alongside Derby Works. (Mike Jefferies/Rail Photoprints)

Above: With its celebrity status came an ironic repaint into two-tone green livery followed in 1987 courtesy of Holbeck Depot, culminating in preservation after this run on 16 February 1991 seen at Hellifield nearly four years after the Class 25s were officially withdrawn. (Rail Photoprints)

Opposite: In 1984 the same locomotive, now as No. 25322, was chosen as part of the Tamworth Rail Week celebrations, gaining this attractive paint scheme at Tyseley as a result and a celebrity was born, affectionately known as the Ice Cream Van. Late in 1985 a small fleet of Class 25s was chosen to be designated Class 25/9 for implementation of the first sectorisation idea. This sub-class were restricted to 60 mph to minimise traction motor problems and they were authorised to receive 'E' exams. The traffic flows planned for the Class 25/9s did not reach the expected levels so the sub-class migrated back to normal duties, losing their special mechanical attention. Whilst the remainder of the Class 25/9s were all still in standard blue liveries, No. 25322 became No. 25912 seen here at Springs Branch on 5 April 1986. (Strathwood Library Collection)

Double-Headers

Above: The beauty of Mid-Wales is shown to good effect with Nos 25305 and 25194 coasting down from Talerddig with the 10.10 Euston–Aberystwyth train at Commins Coch on 4 June 1983. After withdrawal on 17 June 1985, No. 25194 was to be sentenced to a long wait before final scrapping. Firstly, No. 25194 was stored at Shrewsbury's Coton Hill Yard from June 1985 until a move to Bescot on 29 August 1986. After a lengthy wait in the yard alongside the M6 motorway until 28 March 1994, it was finally moved by road to MC Metals Processing in Glasgow, and was scrapped there by the first week of May 1994. (Steve Burdett)

Opposite: This duo of Nos 25170 and 25215 make a pleasant sight and sound as they chatter past Aller Junction with a westbound ballast spoil train in the sunshine of 7 June 1976. (Dave Cobbe Collection/Rail Photoprints)

Another brace of Class 25s attracts the attentions of the platform-enders at Aberystwyth on 7 May 1984. This was a Wessex Railtours organised special from Swindon called The Cambrian Crusader utilising Nos 25154 and 25209 on the legs from Birmingham New Street to here and back. Interestingly, this tour train doubled as a service train between Shrewsbury and Aberystwyth in both directions, forming the 10:55 to Aberystwyth going out and the 17:05 return to Shrewsbury. (Tim Hall)

Above and below: Road traffic appears to be light on the approaches to Abergavenny on 23 August 1980 as this pairing of Nos 25042 and 25221 has charge of Crewe to Cardiff service. Entering Birmingham's New Street station from the approach tunnels with a Sundays-only Walsall–Great Yarmouth working on 14 July 1979 for a hopefully pleasant day at the seaside are Nos 25038 and 25153. (Photos: Steve Burdett)

Leaning into the curve skirting the Dovey Estuary are Nos 25037 and 25048 at Glandyfi near Machynlleth, with the 07.50 Euston–Aberystwyth on 21 July 1984. (Rail Photoprints)

Rats on Heat

When the former D7660, now running as No. 25310, was withdrawn in October 1982 at Tyseley with bogie damage it could have been expected to gain a one-way ticket to Swindon Works. However, late in December it found its way to Aberdeen Ferryhill, where the local staff converted the machine to a non-powered electric-generator vehicle, allocated the number ADB No. 97250 and named ETHEL 1. The use of Mk III sleepers on the Fort William service had caused an operational dilemma as this service was worked by steam-heat 37/0s and the 37/4 conversions were was still some way off. In light of these changes, it is not known why the recently released ETH-equipped 27/2s were not utilised for this service. It is seen here at Oxford on 1 November 1988, and it would survive until August 1994, when it was broken up at MC Metals in Glasgow. (Brian Daniels)

Next up we see the former No. 25305 in the now-revised livery for ETHELs and numbered as No. 97251 awaiting her next duty at Fort William on 14 September 1988. By this time, their use coupled inside steam locomotives on specials had given rise to concerns for their windscreens being hit by coal from the tenders, hence the fitting of protection grills. (Arthur Wilson)

Above: Instead of scrapping all of the Class 24s, the Western Region selected Nos 24054 and 24142 to become carriage-heating units in the West Country during 1976. Renumbered as ADB Nos 968008/9 respectively, the former No. 24054 is seen here after some minor surgery, including the fitting of ETH jumpers as the two units took up their new duties at a variety of the region's depots. (Strathwood Libary Collection)

Middle and below: Mid-September 1982 found the now-repainted ADB968008 on the move, headed for Cambridge to replace some of the equally ancient Class 31 heating units. Also moved was ADB968009, the former No. 24142, to provide some spares. The move to Cambridge was shortlived – excessive noise proved onerous to a nearby residential neighbourhood – so by mid-December the Class 24s and the two Class 31s were stored at March and here at Stratford. This tenuous 'life-extension' brought the former No. 24054 to the attention of the preservation movement, who were able to secure it during October 1983, when it reached the East Lancs at Bury, sadly No. 24142 did not, though before its destruction fortunately it yielded many parts for its sisters. (Photos: Grahame Wareham & Strathwood Library Collection)

By the end of September 1983, No. 25314 had reached Aberdeen Ferryhill for completion for its conversion to ETHEL III numbered No. 97252, the following summer it was tucked inside a Class 37 at Fort William on 16 August 1984. For those still wondering what ETHEL stands for Electric Train-Heating Ex-Locomotive. After their work disappeared in early 1992, all three ETHELs returned to Inverness for storage where they remained for the next eighteen months, before being sent to Glasgow for breaking up. (Arthur Wilson)

Rat Traps

After withdrawal, No. 25027 was sent to Swindon Works. However, the works closed before the locomotive was broken up, so on 26 May 1987 it left the works bound for Vic Berry's in Leicester, reaching Hinksey where we see it on 2 June 1987 and Vic Berry, Leicester on 11 June 1987. The full line-up here was Nos 25027/75, 25123/133/144/158, 25228/234, 97202, 40046/63. (Brian Daniels)

Whilst the lead Class 24 of this pairing at Swindon Works for scrapping is numbered as No. 24025, it is thought actually to be a combination of parts from the long-withdrawn D5005, scrapped at Derby Works, and the real D5025, and would be broken up during the following July. (Strathwood Library Collection)

Stripped of anything salvagable, this duo led by No. 24064 stands in the yard at Swindon Works in the summer of 1976. Identifiable chunks of this locomotive were observed after it had been broken-up at this former Great Western Railway's works later on at King's scrapyard in Snailwell near Kings Lynn in late 1979. (Strathwood Library Collection)

With chunks of locomotives such as No. 25204, a collision casualty from 1980, left like this at Swindon on 22 March 1981, it is easy to see how, once transported away, they may still be identified, although the market for collectors and flame cuts might hinder this. (Bob Dibley)

Eleven Class 24s would not survive long enough to gain their TOPS numbers; among that number was No. 5067, which was withdrawn on 9 October 1972 with accident damage. This is the good side, seen at St Rollox on 12 May 1973, it would be cut up by that October. (Rail Online)

As we have mentioned already Vic Berry's of Leicester was one scrap dealer to benefit from the demise of large numbers of first-generation rolling stock. So busy were they that they concentrated on removing the valuable non-ferrous and easy heavy scrap first from the engine bays, frames and bogies, leaving the cabs for another day, as here on 10 July 1987. (Steve Feltham)

Some of those identifiable parts from No. 24064 have caught our photographer's attention in the yard at Swindon on 27 February 1977, perhaps this is what was seen at Snailwell in late 1979? (Strathwood Library Collection)

Not much to identify the wrecked and charred remains of D5028 after the crash at Chester in 1972. Fire damage would put paid to D5088 as well, seen here at Derby Works in August 1971, while it is collision-damage alone that will spell the end for D5131 when it gets to Glasgow Works after this view at Inverness was taken in 1971. (Photos: Grahame Wareham)

On 22 September 1978 No. 25171 was working a ten-wagon ballast train southbound at Arbroath when the train ran out of control and was diverted into the goods yard, since both mainlines were occupied at the time. It demolished the buffer stops and impacted hard onto the retaining wall, causing major structural damage to the locomotive, not helped by two of the now-derailed ballast wagons demolishing the rear of the stricken Class 25. The guard and driver's assistant jumped to safety, the driver taking refuge in the engine room at the point of impact. It was cut up on site by British Rail staff in January 1979, with the remains being transported away to Glasgow Works in February. (Steve Burdett)

Many of the Class 24s stored at Carlisle found their way to Doncaster Works for disposal, such as No. 24010 leading the line here at the nearby depot in August 1976. (Strathwood Library Collection)

Doncaster's cutting staff have already had a few nibbles out of No. 25237 within the works at the time of this view on 20 April 1986. (Strathwood Library Collection)

In the company of Nos 25318 and 08246, the rather unloved hulk of No. 25028 was seen in the summer sunshine on 5 August 1984. It had been withdrawn on the first day of December 1980, spending long periods dumped at Millerhill and Polmadie before arriving here at St Rollox. Three years later, Vic Berry established a small site at Thornton Junction for breaking up the withdrawn locomotives in Scotland. A number of Classes 25/26/27 were moved here, including Nos 25028, 25318, 27016/027 on 29 January 1987. Unfortunately after the discovery of asbestos in some of these locomotives the decision was made to transfer the remaining machines to Leicester for safe processing. After about five months at Thornton Junction Nos 25028, 25318 and 26013 were sent to Leicester, routed Thornton Junction–Mossend–Carlisle–Crewe–Leicester, making their journey in early June, with No. 25028 being finally broken up by the end of that same month. (Strathwood Library Collection)

Still fitted with a hotch-potch of parts, including an early radiator grill and a Class 25 style of headcode surround, No. 24134 patiently awaits its demise along with No. 24079 at Swindon Works on 13 August 1978.

Withdrawn with collision damage on 18 August 1976 was No. 25003, being moved here to Glasgow Works a year before this view was taken on 1 October 1977 and scrapped here the following January.

The five years spent after withdrawal at Eastfield being used as a training and re-railing locomotive have left their marks, along with vandalism, on the ruins of No. 24006 when it was seen at Glasgow Works in 1980 and cut up towards the year's close. (Photos; Strathwood Library Collection)

A general view of Vic Berry's Leicester scrapyard at 6.30 a.m. on the morning of Sunday 14 June 1987, with many Class 25s recently delivered and awaiting stacking prior to their eventual torching. (Gordon Edgar)